HERE COME THE

Fields of Gold —

    Style = 001

    Voice = 065

Wise Publications
part of The Music Sales Group

London / New York / Paris / Sydney / Copenhagen / Berlin / Madrid /= Tokyo

Published by

Wise Publications
14-15 Berners Street, London W1T 3LJ, UK

Exclusive Distributors:

Music Sales Limited
Distribution Centre, Newmarket Road,
Bury St Edmunds, Suffolk IP33 3YB, UK

Music Sales Pty Limited
20 Resolution Drive,
Caringbah, NSW 2229, Australia

Order No. AM996743
ISBN 978-1-84772-971-2
This book © Copyright 2009 Wise Publications,
a division of Music Sales Limited.

Edited by Jenni Wheeler.
Music processed by Paul Ewers Music Design.

Cover designed by Liz Barrand.

Printed in the EU

www.musicsales.com

F#   Retro pop

Rihanna

Disturbia

Words by Christopher Brown, Robert Allen & Andre Merritt
Music by Brian Seals

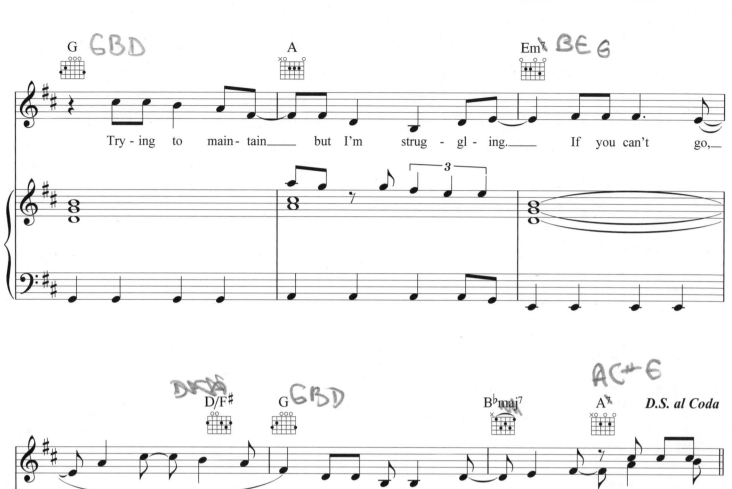

Try-ing to main-tain____ but I'm strug-gl-ing.____ If you can't go,____

think I'm gon-na oh,____ oh, oh,____ oh, oh. Turn on your

⊕ Coda

N.C.

(Bam bam be dam bam__ bam be dam bam. Bam bam be dam bam__ bam be dam bam.)

Vocal ad lib.

9

Lily Allen
The Fear

Words & Music by Lily Allen & Greg Kurstin

12

'Cause I'm____ be - ing ta - ken o - ver by the____ fear.____

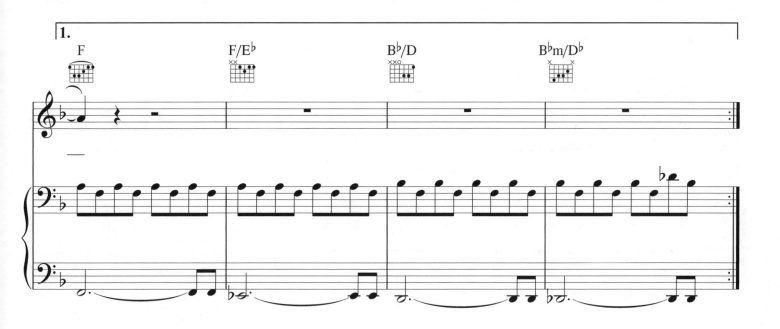

but I'm not a sin - ner, and ev-'ry-thing's cool___ as long as I'm get-ting thin -

D.S. al Coda   Coda

- ner.   And   I   don't   know___

15

Girls

Words & Music by Allen Toussaint, Nicole Jenkinson & Anna McDonald

Here come the girls,

girls,_____ girls. Here come the girls,_____ girls,_____

girls. Here come the girls,_____ girls,_____

girls. Here come the girls,_____ girls,_____ girls.

N.C.

1. Slip-ping on my lit - tle black dress, five inch - es, I'm bound to im - press.
2. Hear the whis - tle as____ I walk by, shine like a crys - tal all____ through the night.

Turn it up, I'm a lit-tle tempt- ress. Oh,___ ooh.___ Mon - roe's got noth-ing on me,
One look-'ll make a grown man cry. Whoa, whoa. Step a side, I got a star - ring role.

read my curves like___ po - et - ry. To - night we rule the world. Be - ware, 'cause
Cam - era, ac - tion,___ here we go. To - night we rule the world. Be - ware, 'cause

1.

here come the girls!_ (Here come the girls.)_

2.

Here come the girls,_ here come the girls!_ Here come the girls,_

Alesha Dixon

The Boy Does Nothing

Words & Music by Nick Coler, Alesha Dixon, Brian Higgins, Miranda Cooper, Timothy Powell,
Carla Williams, Jason Resch & Kieran Jones

28

Alexandra Burke

Hallelujah

Words & Music by Leonard Cohen

Style = 025 =
Voice = 037
Split = Bb
___
Accomp down   Intro on + Synchro on.

Katy Perry

Hot N Cold

Words & Music by Max Martin, Lukasz Gottwald & Katy Perry

Beyoncé

If I Were A Boy

Words & Music by Tobias Gad, Beyoncé Knowles & Britney Carlson

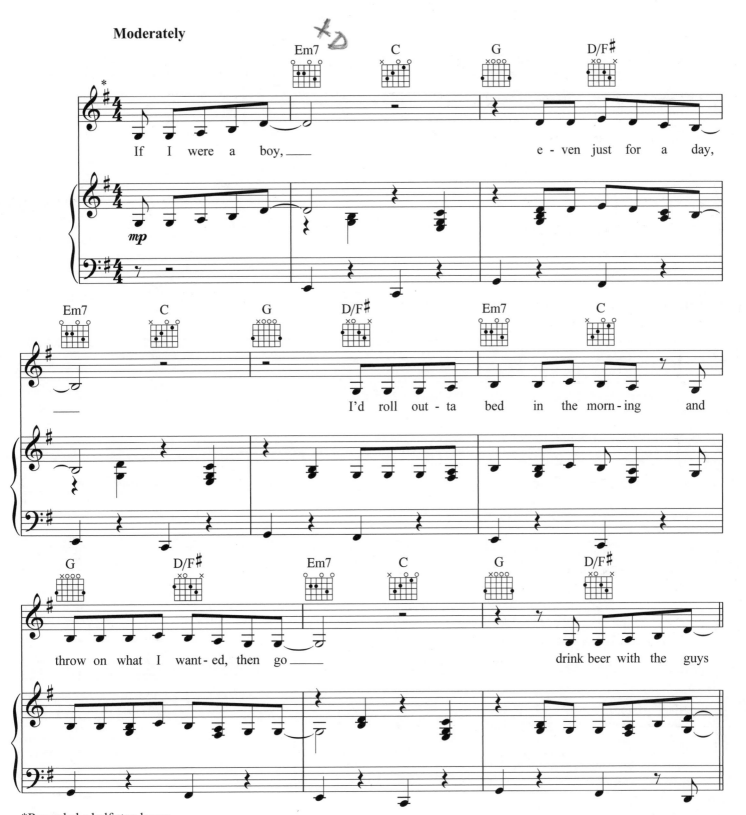

*Recorded a half step lower.

41

47

The Pussycat Dolls

I Hate This Part

Words & Music by Wayne Hector, Lucas, Mich Hansen & Jonas Jeberg

Just Dance

Words & Music by Aliaune Thiam, Stefani Germanotta & Nadir Khayat

but I can't see straight an-y-more.__ Keep it cool. What's the name of this club?__

__ I can't re-mem-ber, but it's al-right, a - al-right. Just

C#m   E   G#m/B   B⁷sus⁴/F#   C#m   E

dance,__ gon-na be o-kay. Da doo doo. Just dance,__ spin that re-cord, babe.

G#m/B   B⁷sus⁴/F#   C#m   E   G#m/B   B⁷sus⁴/F#

Da da doo doo, mm. Just dance,__ gon-na be o-kay. D - d - d - dance.__

58

(Spoken) Let's go!

Half psy-chot-ic, sick, hyp-not - ic, got my blue-print it's sym-phon - ic. Half psy-chot-ic, sick, hyp-not-

-ic, got my blue-print e - lec-tron - ic. Half psy-chot - ic, sick, hyp-not -

-ic, got my blue-print it's sym-phon - ic. Half psy-chot - ic, sick, hyp-not -

D.S. al Coda

Coda

61

Girls Aloud
The Loving Kind

Words & Music by Brian Higgins, Chris Lowe, Neil Tennant, Miranda Cooper & Timothy Powell

68

Adele
Make You Feel My Love

Words & Music by Bob Dylan

72

to make you feel my love.

Duffy

Rain On Your Parade

Words & Music by Stephen Booker & Duffy

I hope you live,— oh, ba - by,— so I can watch you cry.—

'Cause I know— in time you'll see— what— you did— to me

and you'll come run-ning back.— I'm gon-na rain on your—

— pa - rade. No, I won't take it a - gain.

Em

B

75

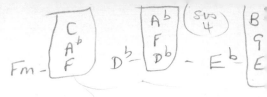

Run

Leona Lewis

Words & Music by Gary Lightbody, Jonathan Quinn,
Mark McClelland, Nathan Connolly & Iain Archer

Jennifer Hudson

Spotlight

Words & Music by Mikkel Eriksen, Tor Erik Hermansen & Shaffer Smith

86

89

Rock Shuffle

Pink

So What

Words & Music by Max Martin, Alecia Moore & Johan Schuster

na na na na na na. Na na na na na na na na na na na na na. 1. I

guess I just lost my hus - band, I don't know where he went. So I'm gon-na drink my mo - ney, I'm
(2.) wait-er just took my ta-ble and gave it to Jes-si-ca Simps... I guess I'll go sit with drum boy, at

not gon - na pay his rent.
least he'll know how to hit.

I got-ta brand new at-ti-tude and I'm gon-na wear it to-night.
What if this song's on the ra-di-o, then some-bod-y's gon-na die.

I'm gon-na get in trou - ble,
I'm gon-na get in trou - ble, my ex will start a fight.

I wan-na start a fight.
Na na na na na na na.

I wan-na start a fight.
He's gon-na start a fight.

Na na na na na na na.
Na na na na na na na. We're all gon-na get in a fight. } So,

94

96

The Saturdays
Up

Words & Music by Andreas Romdhane, Josef Larossi & Ina Wroldsen

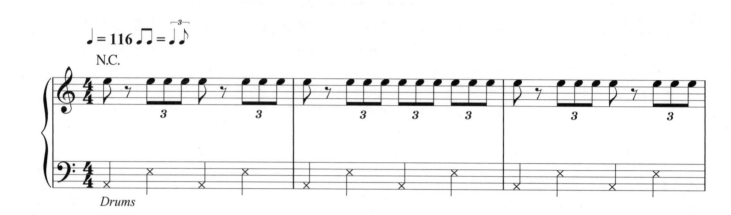

Britney Spears
Womanizer
Words & Music by Nikeshia Briscoe & Rapheal Akinyemi

1. Su - per - star, where you from, how's it go - ing?_ I know you got a
2. Dad - di - o, you got the swag - ger of a cham - p'on. Too bad for you, you just can't

Boy, don't try to front, I, I know just, just what you are, are, are.

F#m   C#m/E

You say I'm cra - zy,   I got your cra - zy,

Eb   D   To Coda ⊕

you're noth - ing but   a   wom - an - iz - er.

A   C#m

May - be if we both lived in a diff-'rent world,_____

123456789